The SUPREMACY of Christ

A 6-WEEK STUDY OF PAUL'S LETTER TO THE
COLOSSIANS AND LESSONS FOR THE MODERN CHURCH

LATISHA J. LEE

Scripture passages are taken from the Christian Standard Bible®

Christian Standard Bible® Copyright © 2017 by Holman Bible Publishers. Used by permission, all rights reserved

ISBN: 979-8-218-83427-2

www.latishajlee.com

The Supremacy of Christ: A Study of Paul's Letter to the Colossians and Lessons for the Modern Church

Throughout history, culture has shaped our understanding of who Jesus is, what He has done, why He exists, and where creation stands in relation to Him. This study aims to help us gain an accurate view of Christ.

If Jesus is Lord of all, our knowledge of His supremacy should inform:

- Our witness (how we live)
- Our understanding of Scripture
- Our identity as the church
- Our relationship with our neighbor

This is a 6-week study of Paul's letter to the Colossian church with lessons for the modern church.

CONTENTS

Latisha J. Lee is a mom to Darryle, Jacob, and Jalyn Faith. She is a Bible teacher, daughter, sister, niece, cousin, and friend. She loves the Lord, who has transformed her heart toward loving His church and His Word.

BEFORE YOU GET STARTED

Thank you. I pray your knowledge of Jesus will deepen as you draw closer to Him through studying the Word and the testimonies found in Scripture.

Each week is broken down into three sections:

- **Observation**: Read the selected passage of Scripture from Colossians. Take time to reflect on what you read, writing down questions and asking the Holy Spirit to help you understand it. Don't rush this part—take time to meditate on what you've read.
- **Interpretation**: Word study, cross-referencing Scripture, and more are encouraged in this section. "Hidden treasures" are often revealed when we search the Scriptures. Explore, be curious, and think critically.
- **Reflection**: This section is provided for worship, repentance, and prayer. Allow the Lord to search your heart and reveal areas that need pruning or nurturing.

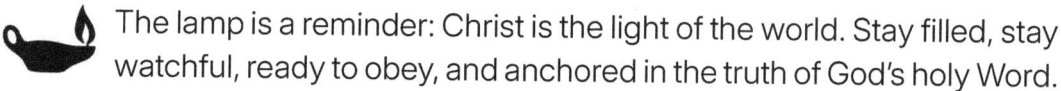 The lamp is a reminder: Christ is the light of the world. Stay filled, stay watchful, ready to obey, and anchored in the truth of God's holy Word.

Useful biblical resources: Expository dictionary, commentary, and study Bible

Helpful online tools: www.blueletterbible.com, www.logos.com

INTRODUCTION

I sat on the other side of the screen, listening as the teacher read:

"He is the image of the invisible God, the firstborn over all creation. For by Him all things were created that are in heaven and that are on earth, visible and invisible, whether thrones or dominions or principalities or powers. All things were created through Him and for Him" (Colossians 1:15–16).

Jesus is not just my Savior and Keeper—He is God. The One who suffered yet reigns with all power and wisdom. I always knew Jesus as divine, co-equal, and co-eternal with the Father. However, the Holy Spirit gripped me with those poetic words from Paul to the church in Colossae. My eyes were opened, and my heart renewed. I would never read Scripture the same way again. Sermons and teachings that did not point to or elevate Christ became dull to my ears.

Years later, while teaching this text, I told the ladies in my Sunday school class that I would write a study on the supremacy of Christ. My prayer is that as you walk through this study, your heart will be captivated by the supremacy of Christ. May you be filled with the knowledge of who He is—not just in history, but in this very moment. There is nothing greater—no created thing, seen or unseen—that can compare to the majesty of our soon-coming King.

Come with me—let's dive in together.

Held together by His supremacy,

Latisha

WEEK 1

BE FILLED

Culture changes, but God's Word endures.

Although these have a reputation for wisdom by promoting self-made religion, false humility, and severe treatment of the body, they are not of any value in curbing self-indulgence.

— COLOSSIANS 2:23

THIS WEEK'S FOCUS

The influence that culture had on the Jewish and Greek churches.

Influencers and teachers of the time were promoting the idea that tradition, angels, nature, knowledge, diets, asceticism, and other practices were essential to salvation.

"Paul's readers were to base their ethical conduct on the authoritative teaching about Christ. For that reason the apostle warned the Colossians not to be deceived by the 'philosophy' and 'empty deceit' of their opponents, which was according to human tradition, according to the elemental spirits of the world, and not according to Christ."[1]

Why? The church was shifting—adopting and/or adding heretical teaching, as well as popular Greek ideas and philosophies, to the gospel.

 **Watch.** Errors are inevitable, but we should strive to know the truth for ourselves.

---

1 George E. Cannon, "Colossians, Letter to The," Baker Encyclopedia of the Bible (Grand Rapids, MI: Baker Book House, 1988), 498.

COLOSSIANS 1:1–2

Paul, an apostle of Christ Jesus by God's will, and Timothy our brother: **2** To the saints in Christ at Colossae, who are faithful brothers and sisters.

Grace to you and peace from God our Father.

What do you know about Colossians?

Begin by reading Colossians. The letter is divided into four chapters. Try reading it once without the section headings. A heading-free copy is provided on page 83. What stands out? Write, journal, or doodle it here.

As we read scripture, we can trust the Holy Spirit to help us ask questions and understand the text. Here are some initial questions to ask of Colossians 1:1-2.

Who is the writer? Are there multiple writers?

Where was the apostle Paul when he wrote this letter? (Hint: see Colossians 4:3,18.)

Who is he writing to?

Where is the church?

Take note of cross-references and record your observations and questions.

What questions do you have? Ask the Holy Spirit for guidance.

God wants you to know Him. How does He help us understand Scripture?

Read and write **John 14:26** here:

Use a Bible dictionary, lexicon, or other resources to define "apostle" and "saints." The scriptures listed are to get you started. Take note of any others that stand out to you and write them here.

Apostle:

- Luke 6:13:

- Acts 1:21–22:

- Galatians 2:8:

- Hebrews 3:1:

What else did you learn about this word?

Saints:

- Romans 1:7:

- Romans 8:27:

What else did you learn about this word?

According to Scripture, who are saints?

Paul says he is an apostle "by God's will." How can you know the will of God? Do a Bible verse search for "will of God" and illustrate a few of the verses here:

1 Peter 3:17

1 Thessalonians 4:3

The Will of God

Matthew 7:21

Write what you find in Scripture that describes God's will for your life:

Pray and ask the Lord to remove barriers that prevent you from surrendering to His will. Ask Him to help you be obedient to His will.

WALK WORTHY PLEASING HIM

When error is ignored and repentance is absent, heresy takes root.

[3] In him are hidden all the treasures of wisdom and knowledge. [4] I am saying this so that no one will deceive you with arguments that sound reasonable.

—COLOSSIANS 2:3–4

Jesus' relationship with the Father and the dynamic between newly converted Jews and Greeks.

Gentiles—who were once far off—needed to know that they had been brought near by the blood of Christ. God has always had a redemptive plan for all nations, glimpses of which appear in Genesis 12:3 and Galatians 3:8–9.

The Jews were called to trust wholly in the God of their fathers, now revealed as the Father of Jesus Christ.

Psalm 2:7 declares that God begot one Son—the LORD.

Proverbs 30:4 asks a piercing question. The answer is clear: God has a Son, and His Son has a name.

Isaiah 9:6 prophesies the birth of the Messiah—the Son of God.

Hosea 11:1 speaks of God's Son coming out of Egypt, echoed in Matthew 2:14.

Yet even among the converted, distortions arose. The Jewish believers drifted toward legalism and tradition, while Greek converts were drawn to the wisdom and philosophies of their culture. Both groups, shaped by pride and the weight of their histories, needed the same thing: grace and redemption.

Why? *Saints:* The only qualifier for us to be called saints is a relationship with Christ.

Apostles: Jesus referred to the disciples as apostles because they were sent. The apostles qualified themselves as apostles because they were eyewitnesses of Christ's burial and resurrection. Paul noted that apostles also performed signs and wonders and laid the foundation of the church (2 Corinthians 12:12, Ephesians 2:20).

Will of God: We need to know God's will so that we will not be tossed to and fro by worldly philosophies and culture. Culture will change, but He does not!

Pray and read chapter 1 again.

COLOSSIANS 1:3–8

Grace to you and peace from God our Father.

3 We always thank God, the Father of our Lord Jesus Christ, when we pray for you, **4** for we have heard of your faith in Christ Jesus and of the love you have for all the saints **5** because of the hope reserved for you in heaven. You have already heard about this hope in the word of truth, the gospel **6** that has come to you. It is bearing fruit and growing all over the world, just as it has among you since the day you heard it and came to truly appreciate God's grace. **7** You learned this from Epaphras, our dearly loved fellow servant. He is a faithful minister of Christ on your behalf, **8** and he has told us about your love in the Spirit.

Read the verses for this week. Some initial questions to ask are:

Who is God? Why do you think Paul makes this connection between God and our Lord Jesus Christ?

What does Paul identify as the evidence of their hope?

How did Paul learn about the Colossian church? What was he told?

Read Colossians 2:1–7 and 4:7–8,12–13. What do these verses reveal about how Paul heard about the saints and how they received his letter? Write what you learn about the following:

Tychicus:

Epaphras:

Take note of cross-references and record your observations and questions.

In Acts 19:8–10 we learn that Paul boldly spoke in the lecture hall of Tyrannus. He shared the gospel, persuading the audience about the kingdom of God. Tyrannus was located in Ephesus, not far from Colossae, Laodicea, and Hierapolis. All of these cities are in what was called Asia Minor—modern-day Turkey. It is widely believed that Epaphras was part of the audience during this two-year period.

Paul states in verses 3–5 that he always thanks God when he prays because he has heard about the faith, love, and hope of the Colossians.

FAITH in _____

What does Galatians 3:26 say about faith?

LOVE for all the _____

What does John 13:34 say about love?

HOPE laid up for you in _____

What does 1 Peter 1:3–5 say about hope?

What can you do to ensure that you are bearing fruit that encourages others to follow Christ? Do a word or topical search for the following terms and verses:

Submission (John 15:5)

Repentance (Matthew 3:8)

Fellowship (Galatians 6:10)

Pray and ask the Lord to reveal areas where you have not submitted to Him. Write them down here and search for verses, as you did above. Meditate on these verses this week.

BE FRUITFUL IN EVERY GOOD WORK

Prayer acknowledges the supremacy of Christ. Manifesting deceives by placing man on the throne.

[11] In view of this, we always pray for you that our God will make you worthy of his calling, and by his power fulfill your every desire to do good and your work produced by faith, [12] so that the name of our Lord Jesus will be glorified by you, and you by him, according to the grace of our God and the Lord Jesus Christ.

— 2 THESSALONIANS 1:11–12

Pauline prayers.

Take a look at some of the Pauline prayers: Ephesians 1:15–21, Philippians 1:9–11, 2 Thessalonians 1:11–12. What are the similarities and differences? What is Paul asking?

As believers in Christ, we are not bound by time, posture, or location. We are encouraged to pray at all times. The Word of God shows us that prayer connects us to the Lord in a way that benefits us individually and corporately. Prayer is essential and a privilege. We can be assured that the Lord hears our prayers.

Jesus is at the right hand of the Father interceding for us! (Romans 8:34, Hebrews 7:23–25).

Why? *Faith in Christ:* The Levitical laws were suitable for a people who had no idea how to live with and for God. Faith in Christ means trusting Him not only to keep you, fill you, and save you but also to present you faultless before God for eternity. That's why it is pointless or futile to put our trust in anything or anyone that is created or mortal. Our Father is eternal. We can put our faith in Him.

Love for all the saints: We are commanded to love our neighbor. Love one another as He has loved us.

Hope laid up for you in heaven: Our hope comes from the Lord—He gave it to us. He is the author of our hope. It's not a wish, but an expectation that

God will do what He says He will do. He has prepared an eternal home for those who believe.

Watch. By faith, Christ has reconciled you to God. Do not shrink back, saints! You have been given access to the Father. The Word declares it a great reward to enter, by faith and with confidence, the throne of grace to receive mercy. So pray—pray without ceasing to the Father who hears and is able to answer.

Pray and read chapter 4.

WEEK 3

9 For this reason also, since the day we heard this, we haven't stopped praying for you. We are asking that you may be filled with the knowledge of his will in all wisdom and spiritual understanding, **10** so that you may walk worthy of the Lord, fully pleasing to him: bearing fruit in every good work and growing in the knowledge of God, **11** being strengthened with all power, according to his glorious might, so that you may have great endurance and patience, joyfully **12** giving thanks to the Father, who has enabled you to share in the saints' inheritance in the light.

Read the verses. Some initial questions to ask are:

What does it mean to be filled with the knowledge of His will?

Why does he use the phrases "filled with the knowledge of His will" and "increasing in the knowledge of God"?

Does Paul's prayer convey a sense of urgency or concern? Why or why not?

Epaphras reported that heresies were circulating among the churches (Colossians 2:16–19). These teachings diminished the supremacy and authority of Christ. They combined Gnostic philosophies, Greek influences, and asceticism with Jewish and Christian traditions and beliefs. Jesus was presented as an addition to their teachings in this mixed bag of beliefs, not as God nor as holy or supreme.

Use a Bible dictionary, lexicon, or other resources to define the following terms.

- **Orthodoxy:**

- **Heresy:**

Note the difference.

Look at the belief systems and practices below. How does Colossians guard us against trusting in these ideas?

Gnosticism claims that secret knowledge or escaping this realm leads to salvation. **Colossians 1:13** says

Therefore I can trust:

Universalism says all will be saved. **Colossians 1:23** says

Therefore I can trust:

Asceticism says denying physical pleasures earns spiritual favor.
Colossians 2:21-23 says

Therefore I can trust:

Syncretism mixes different religions and philosophical beliefs as an aim at truth. **Colossians 2:8-9** says:

Therefore I can trust:

A mixed bag of beliefs! Take a moment to read Paul's prayer (vv. 9–12) again. Rewrite his prayer, focusing on what he asked for. How might his prayer influence your approach to Scripture, knowledge, and your relationship with Christ?

_____

Spend some time meditating on these verses. Ask the Holy Spirit to reveal any errors or heretical ideas in your heart. Surrender them to the Lord; it is His pleasure to fill you with the knowledge of who He is!

"Walk worthy of the Lord, fully pleasing to Him" (Colossians 1:10).

Read Colossians 2–4:6 again. Highlight the exhortations and underline the warnings Paul gives to the church in these chapters. Write some of them here. For additional help, read: 2:6–8; 3:1–23; 4:2, 5–6.

EXHORTATIONS	WARNINGS

Pray to remain steadfast in prayer, rooted and built up in Him, being watchful and fully pleasing to Him.

INCREASE IN THE KNOWLEDGE OF GOD

No one can claim knowledge of hidden truths about God and His kingdom beyond what He has revealed in His Word.

The hidden things belong to the Lord our God, but the revealed things belong to us and our children forever, so that we may follow all the words of this law.

— DEUTERONOMY 29:29

Christ's deity.

Paul speaks of Him as the creator, the beginning, and preeminent. He is superior in person, power, deity, and in all He is and all He does.

Why? *The list of terms:* If we are not clear on the truth about prayer, doctrine, and the person of Jesus, then practices like manifesting, whipping yourself with chains, and unbalanced theologies—such as all grace, all faith, and all works—will lead us astray. Jesus can't be superior if you believe that setting your intentions and manifesting your career or spouse is the way to go. Jesus isn't all in all if self-punishment or self-deprivation is seen as a means to righteousness.

Why? *Asceticism:* The false teachers were imposing strict rules about what and how much to eat, drink, and how to treat their bodies.

Why? *Syncretism:* They were blending Christianity with various traditions and philosophies.

Watch. Jesus is not acknowledged as Lord in many spaces. In some, it's the flag; in others, human rights, race, money, or status have taken His place.

The Bible contains 66 books of God-breathed truth given to man and spans approximately 1,500 years. Through revelations, prophecy, and foreshadowing, it all points to one person: Jesus. If the entire Bible magnifies Him—from Genesis to Revelation—then He must be exalted in our churches. We have a responsibility to magnify Christ, the Living Word, who is altogether authoritative and trustworthy.

Ask the Lord to reveal where He has become secondary.

Pray and read chapter 3.

WEEK 4

13 He has rescued us from the domain of darkness and transferred us into the kingdom of the Son he loves. **14** In him we have redemption, the forgiveness of sins. **15** He is the image of the invisible God, the firstborn over all creation. **16** For everything was created by him, in heaven and on earth, the visible and the invisible, whether thrones or dominions or rulers or authorities—all things have been created through him and for him. **17** He is before all things, and by him all things hold together. **18** He is also the head of the body, the church; he is the beginning, the firstborn from the dead, so that he might come to have first place in everything.

Read the verses. Some initial questions to ask are:

Am I completely free from the domain of darkness?

What are the invisible things He created?

Why did Paul use terms like "before," "head," "beginning," "firstborn," and "preeminent" to describe Christ, the beloved Son? Is there a distinction among these terms?

Why was it important for Paul to say *all* things?

Take note of cross-references and record your observations and questions.

He is the visible manifestation of the uncreated, invisible God. God is not a creation of anything. He doesn't derive any attributes from anything to be God.

Mountains and atoms, birds and angels, seen and unseen, were created through His perfect imagination. Christ is all-sufficient. He lacks nothing. Knowledge, time, ideas, and more all come from Him. There is no limit to His understanding, inventiveness, or ingenuity. He exceeds creation's greatest imagination. People look to the stars, stones, angels, and mystics for knowledge or secrets instead of to Jesus, who is before all things and in whom all things consist and are held together!

Jesus is God.

Image of the _____

Firstborn _____

All things were created _____

All things were created _____

He is before _____

In Him all _____

He is the head _____

He is _____

He is the _____

Preeminent or first place in _____

He is before all things, and **by him all things hold together**

Read Colossians 2–3 as you complete the sentences below. Reflect on **the supremacy of Jesus**—who existed before creation and by whom all things are held together.

✦ Colossians 2

2:3 In him are hidden _____

2 9 For the entire fullness _____

2:14 _____ the certificate of debt, with its obligations, that was against us, and has taken it away by nailing it to the cross.

2:16a-17 Therefore, don't let anyone judge you in regard of food and drink. These are a shadow of what was to come:

_____

✦ Colossians 3

3:1 So if you have been raised _____

3:3 For you died, and your life is hidden with _____

_____

3:4 _____,
who is your life, appears then you also will appear with him in glory.

3:11 _____ there
is not Greek and Jew, circumcision, barbarian, Scythian, slave and free; but

_____

3:17 And whatever you do, in word or in deed, do everything in the name _____, giving thanks to God the Father through

_____

Because Jesus is God:

I can trust that He can

I believe He is

I declare that He alone is

I will

The saints of the church in Colossae encouraged Paul with their faith in Christ, the love the diverse body had for one another, and the truth that was bearing fruit. However, heresies threatened the church. Take some time to think about how they could have guarded themselves against these threats.

How will you guard yourself against the ideals, philosophies, and idols that seek to take you captive?

_____

You are my Lord and God! You alone are worthy to receive glory and honor and power, because You have created all things, and by Your will they exist and were created. (Revelation 4:11)

STRENGTHENED WITH ALL MIGHT

Jesus is all-sufficient. He alone is worthy and able to present us faultless before the Father.

The Word became flesh and dwelt among us. We observed his glory, the glory as the one and only Son from the Father, full of grace and truth.

— JOHN 1:14

Christit.

He alone has the power, preeminence, and provision to satisfy the necessity of the cross.

Why? *Invisible God:* Though surrounded by images of gods—crafted by human imagination and hands—we are called to trust in Christ alone. Only He fulfills the Word, and only He can make the claim.

Why? *Firstborn over all creation:* If you don't recognize that He was first, He will be seen only as a figure in history—a prophet, a good person, or some other entity.

Why? *His preeminence* sets Him apart from anything material, confined by time, space, or the grave. He can't be energy—He created it. He can't be an angel—He's superior to angels.

 **Watch.** God's Word is final, true, and the ultimate authority.

In

Genesis 3:15: God prophesied that His SEED would crush the enemy's head.

Daniel 7:13–14: The Ancient of Days gives Christ dominion.

Hebrews 1: Christ is the heir, creator, the radiance of God's glory, the exact representation of God, sustains all things, and is superior to the angels!

Colossians 2:9: In Him is the entire fullness of God's nature!

The Cross

Jesus canceled our debt by setting aside its legal demands. He disarmed the rulers and authorities, putting them to open shame. Through the cross, all who put their faith in Christ are made dead to their trespasses and alive with Him.

Christ alone satisfied our need for an advocate and reconciler. He bridged the chasm created by the Fall.

There is only one Mediator between God and humanity—Jesus Christ. Any system, belief, or tradition that bypasses His lordship, no matter how sincere, falls short of salvation.

No spiritual leader, no matter how esteemed, can forgive sins. They may intercede, they may pray, but they cannot take the place of the cross.

Striving to fulfill the law or earn righteousness through works leaves grace behind. But Scripture says, "While we were still sinners, Christ died for us" (Romans 5:8). He met us in our sin—undeserved, unearned. That is the gospel. Only Jesus saves. He is sufficient!

So ask the Lord to expose anything or anyone you've placed in the space only He can fill. Salvation is not a system; it is a free gift from God by grace.

WEEK 5

COLOSSIANS 1:19–20

19 For God was pleased to have all his fullness dwell in him, **20** and through him to reconcile everything to himself, whether things on earth or things in heaven, by making peace through his blood, shed on the cross.

Read the verses. Some initial questions to ask are:

Is *all the fullness* of Christ reflected in every area of my life?

What needs to be reconciled in heaven?

Why did He need to make peace through the blood of the cross?

Christ is not a Frankenstein of ideas, myths, and beliefs. Neither is He impotent, needing to be propped up by man's influence. He is totally and fully God! The whole earth is filled with His glory. He is full of grace and truth. There are no secrets or hiding places where man can retreat—He fills heaven and earth. He is the reason we marvel at the faithful and are spurred on by the apostles. The peace we needed with God was achieved by Him on the cross. Christ is the hero, the victor, and the lamb. It all points to Him: His wisdom, His power, His authority, His grace, His deity.

Use a Bible dictionary, lexicon, or other resources to define the following terms:

Fullness:

Dwell:

Hypostatic Union:

Incarnation:

How does your understanding of these terms—*fullness, dwell, incarnation, hypostatic union, and incarnation*—protect against false teachings that diminish Christ's supremacy or humanity?

In John 14:6, Jesus says, "I am the way, the truth, and the life. No one comes to the Father except through me." Yet humanity attempts to usurp Christ's power through legalism, asceticism, vain philosophies, and self-made religions.

Let's take an open-book test. I know, I know. Sometimes those are harder than actual tests, but it will be rewarding. Using only the letter to the Colossians, briefly explain how *knowledge, wisdom, intimacy, righteousness,* and *faith* can be perverted to undermine the sufficiency of Christ. Then, write a verse that confronts or corrects the perversion.

How can knowledge be perverted?

Write a verse from Colossians that corrects that error.

How is wisdom used to pervert the truth?

Write a verse from Colossians that sheds light on that deception.

How is intimacy perverted?

Write a verse from Colossians that sheds light on this distortion.

How can righteousness be perverted?

Write a verse from Colossians that corrects this error.

How is faith perverted?

Write a verse from Colossians that reveals this compromise.

Which of these distortions do you most need to guard against in your own walk? How does Colossians call you back to Christ's sufficiency?

An eloquent and compelling lie is still a lie. Those who tell them are "waterless clouds carried along by winds; trees in late autumn—fruitless, twice dead and uprooted. They are wild waves foaming up their shameful deeds; wandering stars for whom the blackness of darkness is reserved forever" (Jude 1:12c–13). Saints, beware of lofty speech.

Take some time to reflect on all you've learned. Think back to moments when you did not depend on the sufficiency of Christ or the gift of salvation.

Do you know anyone who depends on their works to testify to their righteousness? Pray for them and ask the Lord to search your heart for areas that have not yet been fully surrendered.

GIVE THANKS

Glory, honor, dominion, and power all belong to the one who was, who is, and who is to come—Jesus Christ!

3 Grace to you and peace from God the Father and our Lord Jesus Christ, 4 who gave himself for our sins to rescue us from this present evil age, according to the will of our God and Father. 5 To him be the glory forever and ever. Amen.

— GALATIANS 1:3–5

We need Christ as our Savior and Redeemer.

Because He became fully man, Jesus empathizes with our weaknesses—He understands our struggles. And because He is fully God, He has the power to address those struggles: to work them for our good, walk with us through them, renew our minds, and transform us.

Why? *The fullness:* Christ is not lacking in power or authority. The fullness of God dwells in Him completely. He surpasses every tradition and law!

Paul made it clear:

- Jesus is God (1:19–22).
- Jesus created the world (1:15–16)—material and non-material things, seen and unseen.
- Jesus is our reconciler.
- Jesus is greater than angels! (2:18).

Jesus fulfilled the law. Dietary laws and traditions are not required, and those things don't change hearts! The Holy Spirit does.

Why? *Incarnation* and *Hypostatic Union:* Though others have claimed divinity, only Christ's claim—to be fully God and fully man—is upheld by fulfilled prophecy, historical evidence, archaeological discoveries, and over a millennium of transformed lives. He alone is proven to be who He said He was: the Son of God, *"the Word was with God, and the Word was God"* (John 1:1)—sinless, co-eternal, and co-equal within the Trinity.

Watch. Paul highlighted the stark contrast between faith in Christ principles of Gnosis. While Gnosis emphasizes knowledge, morality, and human reason, its followers rely on an intellectual pursuit anchored in self—whereas faith in Christ calls for dependence on divine revelation and the all-sufficiency of God.

Warnings from 1 Corinthians

The message of the cross is considered foolish by those who are perishing, but to those being saved, it is the power of God (1:18).

The world, through its own wisdom, did not know God (1:21).

The Jews request a sign, and the Greeks seek after wisdom (1:22).

Faith should not be in the wisdom of men, but in the power of God (2:5).

The wisdom of the rulers of this age will come to nothing (2:6).

The wisdom of this age is foolishness in God's eyes (3:19).

The Hope We Have in Christ

We were once alienated, once hostile in mind, enemies of God, doing evil deeds (Colossians 1:21).

A doctrine based on works doesn't claim this hope.

A doctrine based on love alone doesn't hold fast to this truth.

A doctrine that doesn't esteem Jesus as God will fail to teach the power of this promise.

Wisdom and persuasive speech won't acknowledge the evil or embrace the redemption and reconciliation Christ achieved for us on the cross. Christ presents us holy and blameless. There is no other name or means by which we can be presented before Him.

Our lives may include suffering—suffering from our sin and growth—dying to ourselves for His glory.

Paul's suffering—his testimony—benefited both them and us!

Reflect and pray.

COLOSSIANS 1:21–23

21 Once you were alienated and hostile in your minds as expressed in your evil actions. **22** But now he has reconciled you by his physical body through his death, to present you holy, faultless, and blameless before him— **23** if indeed you remain grounded and steadfast in the faith and are not shifted away from the hope of the gospel that you heard. This gospel has been proclaimed in all creation under heaven, and I, Paul, have become a servant of it.

Read the verses. Some initial questions to ask are:

Why was it important for Paul to mention that they were "once alienated and hostile in your minds as expressed in your evil actions"?

What hope is available to those who remain steadfast in their faith?

Take note of cross-references and record your observations and questions.

Paul now turns his attention to this church. You were once alienated and enemies of God because of your choices, yet Christ has reconciled you. You are reconciled as a result of the death of Christ. He did this so that you could be presented as holy, blameless, and above reproach. Continue to follow the truth. Persevere in the gospel. Stay grounded, steadfast, and anchored in the hope you heard.

Use a Bible dictionary, lexicon, or other resources to define the following terms:

Apostasy:

Reconciled:

Steadfast:

Let's go a little deeper.

How does Jude 24 support our reconciliation with God?

What confidence does 2 Corinthians 4:14 offer believers?

How does Galatians 2:16 help build our faith and exalt Christ?

What does Hebrews 3:14 encourage us to do to remain steadfast in our faith?

How does Isaiah 55:8–9 remind us of our humanity and His authority and wisdom?

How do 2 Peter 1:16–2:12 help us identify truth from fallacies?

Who holds the final authority over all Scripture according to Revelation 22:16–19?

Lord of All

The inerrant Word of God tells us that He was in the beginning, that all things were created through Him and for Him, and that it pleased the Father for the fullness of God to dwell in Him. We should read Scripture with Christ in mind.

Holy Scripture is His story. In it, we find Him. Learn of Him!

Be cautious of those who define God based on human logic.

Let no one convince you that traditions or rituals are of utmost importance.

Resist new ideas and philosophies that make false theological claims.

Knowing what you know, write a letter sharing your observations of the supremacy of Christ within your circle of influence. Where do you see a lack of acknowledging Christ as "Lord of all" in your community, church, or family?

COLOSSIANS

1 Paul, an apostle of Christ Jesus by God's will, and Timothy our brother:

2 To the saints in Christ at Colossae, who are faithful brothers and sisters.

Grace to you and peace from God our Father. **3** We always thank God, the Father of our Lord Jesus Christ, when we pray for you, **4** for we have heard of your faith in Christ Jesus and of the love you have for all the saints **5** because of the hope reserved for you in heaven. You have already heard about this hope in the word of truth, the gospel **6** that has come to you. It is bearing fruit and growing all over the world, just as it has among you since the day you heard it and came to truly appreciate God's grace. **7** You learned this from Epaphras, our dearly loved fellow servant. He is a faithful minister of Christ on your behalf, **8** and he has told us about your love in the Spirit.

9 For this reason also, since the day we heard this, we haven't stopped praying for you. We are asking that you may be filled with the knowledge of his will in all wisdom and spiritual understanding, **10** so that you may walk worthy of the Lord, fully pleasing to him: bearing fruit in every good work and growing in the knowledge of God, **11** being strengthened with all power, according to his glorious might, so that you may have great endurance and patience, joyfully **12** giving thanks to the Father, who has enabled you to share in the saints' inheritance in the light. **13** He has rescued us from the domain of darkness and transferred us into the kingdom of the Son he loves. **14** In him we have redemption, the forgiveness of sins. **15** He is the image of the invisible God, the firstborn over all creation. **16** For everything was created by him, in heaven and on earth, the visible and the invisible, whether thrones or dominions or rulers or authorities— all things have been created through him and for him. **17** He is before all things, and by him all things hold together. **18** He is also the head of the body, the church; he is the beginning, the firstborn from the dead, so that he might come to have first place in everything. **19** For God was pleased to have all his fullness dwell in him, **20** and through him to reconcile everything to himself, whether things on earth or things in heaven, by making peace through his blood, shed on the cross.

21 Once you were alienated and hostile in your minds as expressed in your evil actions. **22** But now he has reconciled you by his physical body through his death, to present you holy, faultless, and blameless before him— **23** if indeed you remain grounded and steadfast in the faith and are not shifted away from the hope of the gospel that you heard. This gospel has been proclaimed in all creation under heaven, and I, Paul, have become a servant of it.

24 Now I rejoice in my sufferings for you, and I am completing in my flesh what is lacking in Christ's afflictions for his body, that is, the church. **25** I have become its servant, according to God's commission that was given to me for you, to make the word of God fully known, **26** the mystery hidden for ages and generations but now revealed to his saints. **27** God wanted to make known among the Gentiles the glorious wealth of this mystery, which is Christ in you, the hope of glory. **28** We proclaim him, warning and teaching everyone with all wisdom, so that we may present everyone mature in Christ. **29** I labor for this, striving with his strength that works powerfully in me.

Chapter 2 For I want you to know how greatly I am struggling for you, for those in Laodicea, and for all who have not seen me in person. **2** I want their hearts to be encouraged and joined together in love, so that they may have all the riches of complete understanding and have the knowledge of God's mystery— Christ. **3** In him are hidden all the treasures of wisdom and knowledge.

4 I am saying this so that no one will deceive you with arguments that sound reasonable. **5** For I may be absent in body, but I am with you in spirit, rejoicing to see how well ordered you are and the strength of your faith in Christ.

6 So then, just as you have received Christ Jesus as Lord, continue to walk in him, **7** being rooted and built up in him and established in the faith, just as you were taught, and overflowing with gratitude.

8 Be careful that no one takes you captive through philosophy and empty deceit based on human tradition, based on the elements of the world, rather than Christ. **9** For the entire fullness of God's nature dwells bodily in Christ, **10** and you have been filled by him, who is the head over every ruler and authority. **11** You were also circumcised in him with a circumcision not done with hands, by putting off the body of flesh, in the circumcision of Christ, **12** when you were buried with him in baptism, in which you were also raised with him through faith in the working of God, who raised him from the dead. **13** And when you were dead in trespasses and in the uncircumcision of your flesh, he made you alive with him and forgave us all our trespasses. **14** He erased the certificate of debt, with its obligations, that was against us and opposed to us, and has taken it away by nailing it to the cross. **15** He disarmed the rulers and authorities and disgraced them publicly; he triumphed over them in him.

16 Therefore, don't let anyone judge you in regard to food and drink or in the matter of a festival or a new moon or a Sabbath day. **17** These are a shadow of what was to come; the substance is Christ. **18** Let no one condemn you by delighting in ascetic practices and the worship of angels, claiming access to a visionary realm. Such people are inflated by empty notions of their unspiritual mind. **19** They don't hold on to the head, from whom the whole body, nourished and held together by its ligaments and tendons, grows with growth from God. **20** If you died with Christ to the elements of this world, why do you live as if you still belonged to the world? Why do you submit to regulations: **21** "Don't handle, don't taste, don't touch"? **22** All these regulations refer to what is destined to perish by being used up; they are human commands and doctrines. **23** Although these have a reputation for wisdom by promoting self-made religion, false humility, and severe treatment of the body, they are not of any value in curbing self-indulgence.

Chapter 3 So if you have been raised with Christ, seek the things above, where Christ is, seated at the right hand of God. **2** Set your minds on things above, not on earthly things. **3** For you died, and your life is hidden with Christ in God. **4** When Christ, who is your life, appears, then you also will appear with him in glory.

5 Therefore, put to death what belongs to your earthly nature: sexual immorality, impurity, lust, evil desire, and greed, which is idolatry. **6** Because of these, God's wrath is coming upon the disobedient, **7** and you once walked in these things when you were living in them. **8** But now, put away all the following: anger, wrath, malice, slander, and filthy language from your mouth. **9** Do not lie to one another, since you have put off the old self with its practices **10** and have put on the new self. You are being renewed in knowledge according to the image of your Creator. **11** In Christ there is not Greek and Jew, circumcision and uncircumcision, barbarian, Scythian, slave and free; but Christ is all and in all. **12** Therefore, as God's chosen ones, holy and dearly loved, put on compassion, kindness, humility, gentleness, and patience, **13** bearing with one another and forgiving one another if anyone has a grievance against another. Just as the Lord has forgiven you, so you are also to forgive. **14** Above all, put on love, which is the perfect bond of unity. **15** And let the peace of Christ, to which you were also called in one body, rule your hearts. And be thankful. **16** Let the word of Christ dwell richly among you, in all wisdom teaching and admonishing one another through psalms, hymns, and spiritual songs, singing to God with gratitude in your hearts. **17** And whatever you do, in word or in deed, do everything in the name of the Lord Jesus, giving thanks to God the Father through him.

18 Wives, submit yourselves to your husbands, as is fitting in the Lord. **19** Husbands, love your wives and don't be bitter toward them. **20** Children, obey your parents in everything, for this pleases the Lord. **21** Fathers, do not exasperate your children, so that they won't become discouraged. **22** Slaves, obey your human masters in everything. Don't work only while being watched, as people-pleasers, but work wholeheartedly, fearing the Lord. **23** Whatever you do, do it from the heart, as something done for the Lord and not for people, **24** knowing that you will receive the reward of an inheritance from the Lord. You serve the Lord Christ. **25** For the wrongdoer will be paid back for whatever wrong he has done, and there is no favoritism.

Chapter 4 Masters, deal with your slaves justly and fairly, since you know that you too have a Master in heaven.

2 Devote yourselves to prayer; stay alert in it with thanksgiving. **3** At the same time, pray also for us that God may open a door to us for the word, to speak the mystery of Christ, for which I am in chains, **4** so that I may make it known as I should. **5** Act wisely toward outsiders, making the most of the time. **6** Let your speech always be gracious, seasoned with salt, so that you may know how you should answer each person.

7 Tychicus, our dearly loved brother, faithful minister, and fellow servant in the Lord, will tell you all the news about me. **8** I have sent him to you for this very purpose, so that you may know how we are and so that he may encourage your hearts. **9** He is coming with Onesimus, a faithful and dearly loved brother, who is one of you. They will tell you about everything here. **10** Aristarchus, my fellow prisoner, sends you greetings, as does Mark, Barnabas's cousin (concerning whom you have received instructions: if he comes to you, welcome him), **11** and so does Jesus who is called Justus. These alone of the circumcised are my coworkers for the kingdom of God, and they have been a comfort to me. **12** Epaphras, who is one of you, a servant of Christ Jesus, sends you greetings. He is always wrestling for you in his prayers, so that you can stand mature and fully assured in everything God wills. **13** For I testify about him that he works hard for you, for those in Laodicea, and for those in Hierapolis. **14** Luke, the dearly loved physician, and Demas send you greetings. **15** Give my greetings to the brothers and sisters in Laodicea, and to Nympha and the church in her home. **16** After this letter has been read at your gathering, have it read also in the church of the Laodiceans; and see that you also read the letter from Laodicea. **17** And tell Archippus, "Pay attention to the ministry you have received in the Lord, so that you can accomplish it." **18** I, Paul, am writing this greeting with my own hand. Remember my chains. Grace be with you.

LEADER
GUIDE

Week 1	Week 2
Be prepared to share information about: • The people and location of Colossae • The history of the church • The problem that Paul addresses This study is intended to demonstrate conclusively that Jesus is Lord of all. You will use the Bible and other resources to study and exegete Scripture. **Close with prayer.**	**Discussion:** Share insights and observations from week 1. This week focuses on Jesus' relationship with the Father and the relationship between newly converted Jews and Gentiles. We are also introduced to Epaphras. **Read:** Ephesians 2:11–22, Acts 2:44–47, Philemon 23 **Close with prayer.**
Week 3	**Week 4**
Discussion: Share observations and reflections from week 2. This week's focus is on Paul's prayer. Examine the following Pauline prayers. What similarities and differences do you notice? **Read:** Ephesians 1:15–20, 3:14–21; Philippians 1:9–11; 2 Thessalonians 1:11–12 **Close with prayer.**	**Discussion:** Share observations and insights from week 3. This week focuses on the person and work of Christ in the lives of believers. He is God, greater than everything and over all things. **Read:** Isaiah 9:6; John 1:1, 14, 3:16–18, 10:28–30; 1 Timothy 3:16; Hebrews 1:8 **Close with prayer.**

Week 5	Week 6
Discussion: Take time to share insights from week 4. What did your group learn?	**Discussion:** Reflect on key truths that have been helpful in your growth as a Christian. Feel free to share how God has impacted you through this study.
This week you'll have an opportunity to delve deeper into the supremacy of Christ. Review world religions, beliefs, and modern-day heresies. Who does the world say Jesus is?	As you wrap up, encourage your group to remain anchored in truth. Explain our need for salvation.
Read: Galatians 1:6–9, 3:1–9, 5:1; Hebrews 1:2, 1 John 2:1	**Read:** Isaiah 53:6, Psalm 14:3, Romans 1:18–32, Philippians 2:5–11
Close with prayer.	**Close with prayer.** Ask the Lord to fill your group with the knowledge of His will in all wisdom and spiritual understanding so that they may walk worthy of the Lord, fully pleasing to Him, bearing good fruit and growing in the knowledge of God.

www.ingramcontent.com/pod-product-compliance
Lightning Source LLC
Chambersburg PA
CBHW041539120626
46551CB00019B/2759